OOPS! ACCIDENTAL INVENTIONS

CHOCOLATE CHIP COOKIES

by Catherine C. Finan

Consultant: Beth Gambro
Reading Specialist, Yorkville, Illinois

Minneapolis, Minnesota

Teaching Tips

Before Reading

- Look at the cover of the book. Discuss the picture and the title.
- Ask readers to brainstorm a list of what they already know about chocolate chip cookies. What can they expect to see in this book?
- Go on a picture walk, looking through the pictures to discuss vocabulary and make predictions about the text.

During Reading

- Read for purpose. Encourage readers to think about chocolate chip cookies as they are reading.
- Ask readers to look for the details of the book. What happened to take the chocolate chip cookie from an accident to a treat?
- If readers encounter an unknown word, ask them to look at the sounds in the word. Then, ask them to look at the rest of the page. Are there any clues to help them understand?

After Reading

- Encourage readers to pick a buddy and reread the book together.
- Ask readers to name two things that happened when chocolate chip cookies were being developed. Find the pages that tell about these things.
- Ask readers to write or draw something they learned about chocolate chip cookies.

Credits:
Cover and title page, © bhofack2/iStock; 3, © YinYang/iStock; 5, © RichLegg/iStock; 7, © AaronAmat/iStock; 9, © Chronicle/Alamy; 10, © Africa Studio/Shutterstock; 11, © Sean D/Shutterstock; 13, © chas53/iStock; 14, © jane/iStock; 15, © INTERFOTO/Alamy; 17, © Eric Glenn/Shutterstock; 19, © iuliia_n/iStock; 21, © Pixel-Shot/Shutterstock; 22TL, © George Rudy/Shutterstock; 22MR, © NASA/ASSOCIATED PRESS/AP Images; 22BL, © Creative-Family/iStock and © Nastco/iStock; 23TL, © PeopleImages/iStock; 23TM, © photohoo/iStock; 23TR, © KenWiedemann/iStock; 23BL, © South_agency/iStock; and 23BR, © RossHelen/Shutterstock.

Library of Congress Cataloging-in-Publication Data

Names: Finan, Catherine C., 1972- author.
Title: Chocolate chip cookies / by Catherine C. Finan.
Description: Minneapolis, Minnesota : Bearport Publishing, [2023] | Series:
Bearcub books. Oops! accidental inventions | Includes bibliographical
references and index.
Identifiers: LCCN 2022034200 (print) | LCCN 2022034201 (ebook) | ISBN
9798885093422 (library binding) | ISBN 9798885094641 (paperback) | ISBN
9798885095792 (ebook)
Subjects: LCSH: Chocolate chip cookies--History--Juvenile literature.
Classification: LCC TX772 .F545 2023 (print) | LCC TX772 (ebook) | DDC
641.86/54--dc23/eng/20220809
LC record available at https://lccn.loc.gov/2022034200
LC ebook record available at https://lccn.loc.gov/2022034201

Copyright © 2023 Bearport Publishing Company. All rights reserved. No part of this publication may be reproduced in whole or in part, stored in any retrieval system, or transmitted in any form or by any means, electronic, mechanical, photocopying, recording, or otherwise, without written permission from the publisher.

For more information, write to Bearport Publishing, 5357 Penn Avenue South, Minneapolis, MN 55419.

Contents

A Yummy Accident 4

Chocolate Chip Cookies Today 22

Glossary 23

Index 24

Read More 24

Learn More Online...................... 24

About the Author 24

A Yummy Accident

Chocolate chip cookies are a tasty treat.

It is fun to bake them.

How did this yummy **invention** happen?

Say invention like in-VEN-chuhn

The first chocolate chip cookies were made in the 1930s.

They happened by **accident**.

Oops!

Ruth Wakefield had a small hotel.

It was called the Toll House **Inn**.

Ruth made food for people who stayed there.

Sometimes, she made cookies.

One day, Ruth tried making chocolate cookies.

She put chocolate pieces in **dough**.

Say dough like doh

Ruth wanted the chocolate to spread through the cookies.

Instead, it made chocolate chip cookies!

No one had made this kind of cookie before.

Ruth called the new treats Toll House cookies.

People loved them!

Some people even wanted to bake them at home.

Ruth Wakefield

15

Stores started selling chocolate chips.

They were like the pieces in Ruth's cookies.

Soon, people could use her **recipe**, too.

It was on bags of chocolate chips!

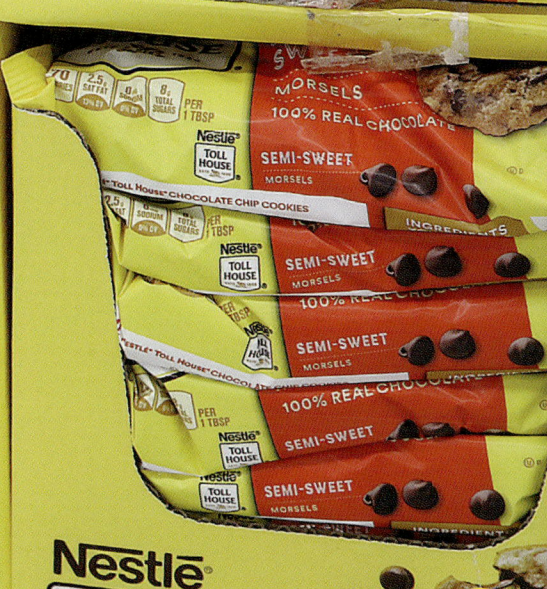

Over time, people made changes to the cookies.

Some used different kinds of chocolate.

Others added nuts or candy.

Today, there are many ways to make these cookies.

And it all started with a yummy accident!

Chocolate Chip Cookies Today

Americans eat 19 million chocolate chip cookies a day.

Chocolate chip cookies were the first food baked in space.

The biggest chocolate chip cookie was huge. It would fill half a hockey rink!

Glossary

accident something that is not planned

dough a mixture that can be baked into cookies

inn a small hotel

invention something new that people have made

recipe a list of steps for making food

Index

accidents 4, 6, 20
dough 10–11
nuts 18
recipe 16
stores 16
Wakefield, Ruth 8–10, 12, 14–16, 18

Read More

Brundle, Harriet. *The Course to Chocolate (Drive Thru)*. Minneapolis: Bearport Publishing, 2022.

Mattern, Joanne. *Chocolate Chip Cookies (Our Favorite Foods)*. Minneapolis: Bellwether Media, 2020.

Learn More Online

1. Go to **www.factsurfer.com** or scan the QR code below.
2. Enter **"Chocolate Chip Cookies"** into the search box.
3. Click on the cover of this book to see a list of websites.

About the Author

Catherine C. Finan is a writer living in northeast Pennsylvania. She has her own secret chocolate chip cookie recipe.